MAKING the End Of IT TO the Month

Discovering and Transforming your Relationship with Money and Possessions

PHILIP BISHOP

DEDICATION

To my amazing children, Hannah and David, and their spouses,
Gareth and Hannah. Most importantly, to Ruth, my wife and
best friend, who has been with me through it all,
sharing all the highs and lows, and still loves me!

ACKNOWLEDGEMENTS

My thanks go to Loulita Gill, Sarah Ansah and Alison Carson who have given me invaluable help and assistance in publishing, proofreading and editing.

I owe an enormous debt of thanks to Rob and Mo James and Ifor and Penny Williams for all the encouragement and help with Generous Heart. Also, for introducing me to these everlasting principles on money – Mark Lloydbottom and Peter Briscoe, you have encouraged me more than you will ever know, thank you.

CONTENTS

Owning our story can be hard but not nearly as difficult as spending our lives running from it. Embracing our vulnerabilities is risky but not nearly as dangerous as giving up on love and belonging and joy – the experiences that make us the most vulnerable. Only when we are brave enough to explore the darkness will we discover the infinite power of our light.

BRENÉ BROWN

INTRODUCTION

Can you imagine a life in which you are able to pay all your bills on time, afford a perfect holiday without having to borrow money and give outrageously to people in need within your community?

Sounds great, doesn't it? But this isn't just a pipe dream. It can become a reality for you. Within the pages of this book, you'll discover financial principles that can put you on the road to financial freedom. Interested? From the outset, let me say that there is no quick-fix. You will need to get serious about understanding and applying these principles. If you do, I guarantee that they will work. The reason I can be so confident is that the financial principles we'll explore in this book are based on biblical teachings and are, therefore, timeless and transcendent regardless of changing economic and world situations.

If you're still interested, then you're about to embark on an exciting journey. Obtaining financial freedom and making it to the end of one month ready to face the next is a constant adventure.

The first two chapters will set the foundation for this important subject. In the following chapters, I'll be asking you to make certain decisions that will change your relationship with money, and that's the ultimate aim of this book. Yes, you read that right. You, like everyone else, have a relationship with money. The way you manage your money depends upon your relationship with it, and that relationship is an indicator of beliefs you hold about yourself, others and the world.

Why should you bother addressing your relationship with money? Well, when that relationship is in order, our relationship with life itself changes. Moreover, our hearts change, becoming generous in nature, not just with money and possessions, but also with time, love, ideas, praise, gratitude, forgiveness and much more. It's a new way of living that requires of us to develop a new perspective on life – and that perspective has everything to do with our relationship with money. This book will help you explore and change your relationship with money, enabling you to make the right decisions about your finances. Daily choices add up over time, and the decisions you'll make through reading this book will set you up for long-term success.

Individuals and couples who embrace a lifestyle of generosity are not merely making it to the end of the month. It is much more than a month-by-month aim of not running out of money. Rather, this lifestyle provides true financial freedom and contentment, plus genuine personal joy.

By engaging fully with this subject and seeking support if required, you will become increasingly conscious of the benefits of generous living. Ultimately, you'll be transformed into a generous person.

I am so pleased you have started this journey. The key is not to stop or give up since this is a life-long adventure. However, this book will prepare you to be attentive to the final destination. Be aware that there may be times when you'll need to re-look at, and perhaps refocus on, the direction you are taking. It's always healthy to re-examine motives and circumstances so that we can change, redirect and then continue on the journey. The skills you will learn can be applied to every area of your life, in all situations, so that you will be able to make it to the end of the month, overcome your money struggles and move towards the holy grail of financial freedom.

Self-care is never a selfish act — it is simply good stewardship of the only gift I have, the gift I was put on earth to offer others. Anytime we can listen to true self and give the care it requires, we do it not only for ourselves, but for the many others whose lives we touch.

PARKER J. PALMER

Let Your Life Speak: Listening for the Voice of Vocation

A PERSONAL NOTE

At the start of this journey, I would like to share with you the source of the principles and values found in this book. I am not the one who has designed or developed these ideas. I believe there is a creator, who is God and Father, and He is the source of all these principles. He created these principles and established them in nature at the very beginning of time. He has offered us, His creation, the opportunity to make them a part of our lives as the fruit of a personal relationship with Him, through His Son and His Holy Spirit.

I also believe God has placed us in a race that we need to run. He has a plan for each one of us. To the degree that we run that race successfully, we fulfil our life's plan and feel more satisfied as individuals.

In writing this book, my desire is not only to help you with your current material experience but also your spiritual one. I hope wholeheartedly that you will be helped to manage and understand your finances in a better way, that your thinking will be transformed, and that you'll develop a generous heart.

Philip Bishop

The world needs dreamers and the world needs doers. But above all, the world needs dreamers who do.

SARAH BAN BREATHNACH

Surround yourself with the dreamers and the doers, the believers and thinkers, but most of all, surround yourself with those who see the greatness within you, even when you don't see it yourself.

EDMUND LEE

CAN'T TAKE IT WITH YOU? | Chapter 1

Summary of short story: 'How Much Land Does a Man Need?'

Written by Leo Tolstoy, 1886

Pahom was a peasant farmer who lived in village. His wife's elder sister came to visit and told her about the good things she could enjoy in the city – good food, clothes, entertainment etc. These things did not lure the farmer's wife. Even though life was not always easy in the village, she was content. She recognised that their life was free and happy away from the temptations of city life.

However, two people overheard the conversation: Pahom, who thought, "If I had plenty of land, I shouldn't fear the Devil himself!" and the devil who took Pahom's thoughts as a challenge and planned to tempt him.

Sometime later, Pahom purchased forty acres of land in the village, thinking it would make him happy. However, instead of discovering happiness, he became very possessive of his land, which caused arguments with his neighbours and resulted in Pahom losing his peace of mind.

After hearing about a prosperous community, Pahom decided to move. But he was dissatisfied living on communal land and desired to own his own property. Finally, he was introduced to the Bashkirs, who owned a huge amount of land. Pahom was told that they were simple-minded people, so he tried to negotiate a good price for as much of their land as he could get.

Their offer was unusual: to sell their land for the sum of 1,000 rubles.

The condition: Pahom had to mark out the land he wanted at that price, but he had to return to his starting point by sunset. Otherwise, he would lose the land and his money.

Pahom's greed was aroused. He believed that he could cover a great distance. He started early the next morning, marking the land with a spade. When he saw the sun starting to set, he headed back, but quickly realised that he was too far from the starting point to make it back in time. He ran as fast as he could, and finally reached the starting point, exhausted. There, he dropped down dead.

Pahom's servant buried him in an ordinary grave only 6-foot long, thus answering the question in the title. "Six feet from his head to his heels was all he needed."

Can't you take it with you?

We all know the answer to this question, and if we were to phrase it as a statement, we'd all agree that 'You can't take it with you' is true. Yet, we still want more.

Why?

Why do we want more? Why are we never satisfied with what we have?

Before we begin to answer this, we need to look at and understand the history of money. We have an excellent saying, 'Money does not grow on trees'. I expect you've heard that said by parents or grandparents. Maybe you have even said it to your own children. The core truth of this saying tells us that money is not a product of nature. In other words, it's a man-made invention. The idea of money was conceived many years ago, and throughout the ages, it has been an acceptable and identifiable method of payment for goods and services, as well as a means to repay debt. Therefore, money is a medium of exchange (a common ground or legal tender) between two or more parties. That's its sole function.

Money itself is a form made of metal or paper (so, technically, the latter does come from trees!), but has also taken other forms in history,

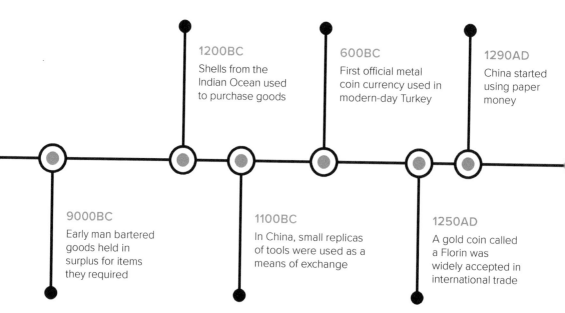

1200BC
Shells from the Indian Ocean used to purchase goods

600BC
First official metal coin currency used in modern-day Turkey

1290AD
China started using paper money

9000BC
Early man bartered goods held in surplus for items they required

1100BC
In China, small replicas of tools were used as a means of exchange

1250AD
A gold coin called a Florin was widely accepted in international trade

e.g., bartering or swapping each other's services. In fact, anything that is acceptable to two parties is a form of exchange and, therefore, can be money. However, the paper and metal version and, now today, the credit version are the most acceptable format. The latest version of money and exchange is bitcoin, an electronic currency.

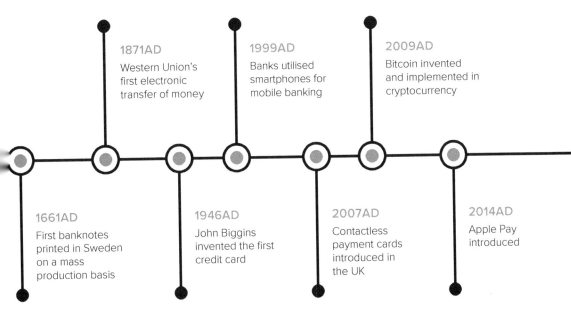

1871AD
Western Union's first electronic transfer of money

1999AD
Banks utilised smartphones for mobile banking

2009AD
Bitcoin invented and implemented in cryptocurrency

1661AD
First banknotes printed in Sweden on a mass production basis

1946AD
John Biggins invented the first credit card

2007AD
Contactless payment cards introduced in the UK

2014AD
Apple Pay introduced

Money in the format we know today is a human invention, as we've seen. Since this is the case, the acceptability of this format relies on one thing and one thing only: TRUST. For example, we trust that our currency is worth the amount engraved or printed on it, and, therefore, we trust that it will be accepted in exchange for goods of the same value. However, if sellers declined our coins and pieces of paper as a means of exchange, they would no longer be acceptable, and we would not trust them. Then, money itself would lose its value. History shows us that humankind will simply replace it with something else, such as the methods already mentioned.

Therefore, money is nothing more than a fabrication of our genius. We have invented the whole concept. It is not real. Every note and coin in our wallets or purses is made-up so that we can exchange services. That includes those plastic credit cards, too! Money is literally made up – we manufacture it. We are so clever that we even create wealth when we have no money. It's called debt. Debt happens when we buy products or services without the ability to pay for them immediately, hoping to repay the deficit over a more extended period. At what cost? It may be more than just the interest rate.

With this understanding of money, let's look at the questions asked earlier more closely. Why do we want always want more money? Why are we never satisfied with what we have? We know for a fact it's not real and that we cannot take it with us, so why do we want more and more of it, even when we are fully satisfied? The answer is simple – money controls us.

Don't believe me? Well, consider this: Our culture as a whole and our lives individually are preoccupied with thoughts about spending money. We devote most of our time to thinking and planning what we will purchase and how we will do so. And as long as people want more and more and more, companies will not only supply the demand but will also formulate ways to sell their merchandise to even more people (those unsuspecting members of the public who didn't know they wanted their product until it was advertised!). Then, in order for more people to make their purchases, more and more money needs to be printed and put into circulation – either to replace damaged currency or to meet demand – until society is in a cycle of spending that is wildly generated by greed.

I realise that may sound harsh, but our starting point on the journey towards generous hearts is recognising and understanding the control of money. The truth is that money demands our attention. For some people, money becomes all-consuming, and chasing it consumes their lives. Sadly, this is not an exaggeration. I gently suggest that this level of obsession is like a cancer that devours and destroys. The effect money has on us can also be likened to a drug – something that controls us rather than us controlling it. If money is so central to our lives that we love it above everything else, then we must learn how to stop this particular drug from consuming us.

Money does talk. It can alienate us from people and life. It can, and will, dominate our every waking moment, whether we have wealth or not. Our culture reinforces this position because we live in a money-driven society. We need to remove this 'cancer of the heart' and then keep it monitored and under control on a regular basis. If we do not, our relationship with money will remain unhealthy and, sooner or later, it will negatively affect the practical, emotional and spiritual areas of our own lives, as well as the lives of our family members. So, it's imperative that we put this relationship right and release the control that money seeks to have over our hearts.

People were created to be loved.
Things were created to be used.
The world is in chaos because things are being loved
and people are being used.

AUTHOR UNKNOWN

Throughout the following chapters, we will consider the immense problem I have described. We will examine why we are unable to control our desire for money, and we'll also discover how to turn the situation around and obtain real peace on this subject.

Before we get going, find a quiet spot, make a cup of tea or coffee, relax, and reflect upon the following:

1. How do you make it to the end of the month?
2. What is your belief system on this critical subject of money?
3. How do you make decisions about buying things?
4. How often do you think about money?
5. Is 'How can I get more?' the only thing you think about?
6. Does money control you or do you control it?

Have you come to the realisation and conclusion that money, and riches associated with money, only have the power that we assign to it? In the majority of our lives, it has become a high power. In fact, we have awarded it total dominance. Having elevated to this level, it has immense power over us, as we saw from the short story by Leo Tolstoy. In some instances, we have given money more meaning than human life. Wherever you are on this scale (and you can be in different positions at different times of your life), the principles you'll learn and the decisions you'll make in this book will help you refocus and put all of life in its proper perspective. In short, it'll help you to make it to the end of the month with a healthy heart and soul.

While you might be in a fantastic financial position at this particular time, it can and may change. In which case, you, too, need to have the tools not to let money dictate the terms of your life.

If you enter this world knowing you are loved and you leave this world knowing the same, then everything that happens in between can be dealt with.

MICHAEL JACKSON (1958 – 2009)

12:07

Don't be impressed by money, followers, degrees, and titles. Be impressed by kindness, integrity, humility, and generosity.

AUTHOR ANONYMOUS

THAT'S THE WAY THE MONEY FLOWS | Chapter 2

"Annual income twenty pounds, annual expenditure nineteen pounds nineteen shillings and sixpence, result happiness. Annual income twenty pounds, annual expenditure twenty pounds ought and six, result misery." Charles Dickens, *David Copperfield*

Understanding how money works will help us figure out the best way to control the money that flows through us, instead of letting money control us. Typically, money will flow in and out of our lives on a weekly or monthly basis either from our salary or from payment for work done. On other occasions, we may receive additional lump sums, such as birthdays, gifts or inheritance. These are infrequent though and are not part of our regular flow. The point is that money comes in and money goes out. Money is always moving.

This free flow of money does make it harder to control. However, whether the flow is like a rushing torrent coming through our lives or a small trickle, we *can* have it in balance and control. In essence, the quantity of money we have is irrelevant; the amount simply helps us to set goals for the financial future we desire.

The quote from Charles Dickens is part of the key to true happiness. Ever since he penned these words in his famous novel, it has been the golden standard for budgeting correctly with the most chance of success.

Yet, we need to go deeper and address our relationship with money. Otherwise, even with the most robust budget and the best intentions in the world, we will revert to old habits that stem from our background, preconceived ideas and any financial education we may have received up until this point. Therefore, to improve our financial situation, we must have the correct controls in place that originate from a proper heart attitude towards money – and this means adjusting our thinking on some matters since our thinking affects our attitudes and behaviour.

John D. Rockefeller (1839 – 1937), the first billionaire in history (in US dollars) said it this way: "The problem isn't the lack of money – it's your thinking about the lack of money."

So, it's clear that the financial problems we face cannot be solved with the same mindset that led to this position in the first place. We need to shift our paradigms and move to a higher level of values and ideas to develop a generous heart that is not controlled by money. The more we adjust our thinking about money, the more our relationship with it will change. This transformation will bring stability and control to the seemingly uncontrollable flow of money.

Now we're going to start the process of saying goodbye to money's domination. In the following chapters, I'll be asking you to make certain decisions that are of paramount importance for your journey to change. Each chapter will begin with, **'I have decided to ...'**

At this juncture, let me re-emphasise that the principles in this book will work only *if* you apply them and only *if* believe them in your heart. So, I encourage you to engage your heart and conscience while reading. Don't read merely to gain information; rather, read with an open mind and heart that desires to be transformed – free from the control of money and, therefore, able to make it to the end of the month successfully.

You must gain control over your money or the lack of it will forever control you.

DAVID L. RAMSEY

Today expect something good to happen to you no matter what occurred yesterday. Realize the past no longer holds you captive. It can only continue to hurt you if you hold on to it. Let the past go. A simply abundant world awaits.

SARAH BAN BREATHNACH

Simple Abundance: A Daybook of Comfort and Joy

WHO OWNS IT ANYWAY? | Chapter 3

I have decided to ... be an administrator.

Look from a different perspective. Do you view yourself as an 'administrator', 'manager' or 'steward' of your talents, gifts, money and possessions?

What do these terms mean? Simply defined, they are all roles that carry the responsibility of caring for something that belongs to somebody else. When we relate this to ourselves, in particular, the area of our finances, it means viewing and treating our money and possessions as not our own, but something for which we are responsible for taking care of and wisely managing.

This is a new perspective about ownership. Since money is a man-made invention and we can't take anything with us, we will never truly own anything. We are only borrowing things. Interestingly, the three most significant religions in the world (Christianity, Judaism and Islam) all have some common ground: they all believe there is a God. Their belief in a creator shapes their conviction that we have been placed in this world to manage the earth and its resources. With this responsibility comes the management of the treasures and riches that are in the world we live, which includes natural riches, such as oil and gold, and invented riches, such as money.

Gaining this insight regarding ownership will change and mould our attitudes, enabling us to see riches as something we do not possess, but something we are just looking after for a certain duration. Indeed, making the decision to be an administrator will serve to reinforce this new perspective of ownership, and it is the first step on the path towards a transformed heart.

Additionally, the choice to renounce ownership of material things will also uncover that our relationship with money is a deeply conflicted one. We start to realise that our values, commitments, ideas and, more significantly, our hearts, affect our behaviour towards money. Therefore, it is essential that we begin the process of cutting all emotional ties to money and possessions so that we can learn to behave like administrators. For this reason, we need to consider what we have and evaluate whether we own it or are just borrowing it. Let me clarify that money in itself is neither good or bad. It is all about the position it takes in our understanding. We need to answer the questions: Who owns it? Is viewing ourselves as an 'owner' a healthy attitude?

When you have reached this point, I hope that you will have realised what genuinely matters to you. A possible conclusion is that you discover your greatest commitment in life and your core value. I suggest that you will end up with the honest desire to become a person who puts others first – someone who is sincerely concerned about the well-being of other people. Already, we can see that the focus of our minds and hearts will have shifted from a self-serving, self-interest in *things* (that we don't own and can't take with us) to a selfless and giving interest in *people* (who make our lives truly rich) and how we can share love with those close to us.

Becoming people-focused rather than money-focused begins with an acknowledgement that we are merely stewards of money and material possessions. It's vital to make this shift in our perspective because people and relationships are infinitely more valuable than anything else. If we want to make it to the end of the month, we must start right here with a quality decision to be an administrator. Actually, we are stewards of many things, and money is only one of those treasures. Our main goal should be to obtain the true riches of life. After that, other goals can include spending, investing, giving and managing our resources and talents.

In a broader sense, this new perspective of ownership can be expanded to our relationships with every person in the world. Even though it's not possible to know everyone personally, we can still extend a people-focused outlook by taking care of the earth in which we live. For example, looking after our environment.

Let's take this one stage further. Most people do not want anything wrong to happen to anyone. Instead, we want to protect others from violence, war or plagues. We want a safe, secure, loving and wholesome life for our families and friends ... and really, for everyone. This is because we are all seeking something beyond the things that money can buy. What is it? When we are true to ourselves, each of us would admit that we want to love and to be loved, to make a difference in this life we have been given. Deep down, it's these lasting experiences we desire, not just temporal ones that can be purchased. And all of this stems back to this first decision to be an administrator since this choice recognises the fact that there is a creator who owns everything and has given us everything, including riches, to manage and take care of. Ultimately, the pinnacle of our journey is to know the creator and to have an authentic relationship with him.

Whatever people say, money cannot buy the joy that comes from this relationship. Yes, having possessions can bring some form of happiness, but happiness is an emotion that will change frequently based on many factors. Therefore, money and possession is not something upon which we should base our lives.

Money is temporary
House is temporary
Car is temporary
Career is temporary
God is eternal

AUTHOR UNKNOWN

You have the power to change how you view money and its uses. Money doesn't own you, neither do you own it. This new perspective will bring about a change in your relationship with money and possessions. Furthermore, when you align your financial decisions with what you've discovered to be meaningful to you, it will change your commitments, and you'll make better choices about how you relate and respond to circumstances. You'll see a dramatic shift in how you handle money and how you feel about it. This is when you'll find that money loses its grip on your heart and reverts to being a method with which to trade. Eventually, you will not be known for what you in your possession, but for what you have given, not for what you have accumulated, but for what you have allocated. You will find out for yourself that generosity is a great way to increase joy, as well as happy emotions.

Make the decision to be an administrator. What will it take? It will require that you stop being self-centred and that you recognise that life is not all about you. This is a simple definition of maturity, and it's neither easy nor comfortable. That is why, unfortunately, some people never mature, even in old age. People who don't mature still hold the perspective that everything is all about them and what they can get. Because they have never matured, they remain in the dangerous grip of money, never disabling its control over them or discovering the joy of generosity. Come on, start the journey of change by making this first decision.

We didn't give ourselves the personalities, talents, or longings we were born with. When we fulfill these — these gifts from beyond ourselves — it is like fulfilling something we were meant to do.

The Creator of all things knows the name of each of us — knows thoroughly, better than we do ourselves, what is in us, for he put it there and intends for us to do something with it — something that meshes with his intentions for many other people. Even if we do not always think of it that way, each of us was given a calling — by fate, by chance, by destiny, by God. Those who are lucky have found it.

MICHAEL NOVAK

Business as a Calling

THE RECIPE FOR CONTENTMENT | Chapter 4

I have decided to ... be content.

Look from a different perspective. You can be content with your lot in life, whether you have little or much. It is entirely possible and attainable to be at peace, to be satisfied, comfortable and at ease with your financial situation. Contentment is not something that comes naturally – we will always want more than we already have. But no matter how much money you have, it will never buy you genuine peace of mind, body and spirit. Real peace, like joy, is not about possessions or circumstances.

The majority of problems associated with money stem from dissatisfaction with our lifestyle. In our culture, we scramble to make that 'social leap' to acquire a bigger house or to purchase something expensive that we are unable to support on current income levels. In the chase for more, we believe the profit-driven commercial and cultural messages that suggest possessions can buy happiness, and we think these material things will satisfy our emotional and spiritual needs, but this is a lie. Only temporary happiness is found down this route. It currently goes by the name of 'materialism'. Money will never bring true happiness to a person's life. In fact, a sudden excessive amount of money often leads to unhappiness because the unexpected wealth captures the person's heart, and they become consumed with it. Money can buy a house, but it can't build a home; it can pay for education, but it can't give wisdom; it can facilitate the means for a heart transplant, but is unable to provide love.

Yet, the dissatisfaction in our souls can be so great that our efforts to make the social leap often come at the expense of our own integrity. We can easily fall prey to dishonesty and corruption in attempts to gain more. This behaviour will become a serious problem because, inevitably, it will affect our own sense of well-being, bringing turmoil to our emotions and relationships. Unfortunately, dissatisfied people do not see their problem or, if they do, they are unable to admit it.

Invariably, we will always want more, but being just as happy with a little as with a lot is a recipe worth aspiring to. In a world dominated by money and an economy that revolves around it, it is vital that we each come off the treadmill of wanting more and more and more, and start developing a thankful heart for what we already have. This is the key to finding contentment and real peace in all economic situations.

Here are some practical steps: Stop comparing yourself to others and stop examining what could be. Instead, consider what you have, notice everything that is in front you and, above all, be thankful. This is challenging, and it will take effort, but the benefit will be great! In the process, you'll find new and profound joy ... personal satisfaction. You can be free from turmoil regarding money and possessions. You can find peace and contentment for your soul.

Consider your routine and then create a method of gratitude and that works for you. You can add things to your day that are achievable. Go on, give it a go and start making it a part of your daily rhythm.

Finally, in chapter seven, we'll discuss the importance of having a spending plan. You can practice the art of contentment by sticking to it. Think of it this way: most people don't get excited about exercising regularly, but by creating disciplines, exercise can become part of a routine. The same is true with a spending plan. Creating one that is flexible enough to work within your individual circumstances will greatly enhance your personal contentment.

Time is more valuable than money. You can get
more money, but you cannot get more time.

JIM ROHN (1930 – 2009)

You can only become truly accomplished at
something you love. Don't make money your
goal. Instead, pursue the things you love doing,
and then do them so well that people can't take
their eyes off of you.

MAYA ANGELOU (1928 – 2014)

PATIENCE IS A VIRTUE | Chapter 5

I have decided to ... be patient.

Look from a different perspective. When your soul is at peace with what you have, you will be able to control the almost constant pressure to buy, buy, buy, spend, spend, spend. This pressure is created by our consumer-oriented society. You will need real patience and conviction to be able to say 'no' to the marketing departments that are pushing you to purchase things you don't really need with money you don't have, to impress people you don't even know or like.

To exercise patience in this important area of money and possessions requires a change in our spending habits. Undoubtedly, it will also require some willpower to start. We will need to reject the prevailing culture of today's market economy and all its advertising, such as so-called offers of 'Buy Now and Pay Later' and special cash-back offers, 'If you buy this item we will pay you a cashback of £x'. Today, as a society, we have acquired more possessions than our ancestors ever did, but in reality, since we purchase nearly everything on credit or using instalment plans, we actually own less.

While we are quick to acknowledge the vicious cycle of outward, physical poverty in our world, we tend to ignore the vicious internal cycle of spiritual poverty. The latter is not recognised since it is camouflaged in apparent wealth, and the cycle is kept in motion by the availability of credit. Yet, it causes suffering for many individuals. Those who are caught in this trap face the potential of loneliness and isolation, with the result of a hardened heart. The spiritual poverty of the soul can become the burden of the 'Buy Now' culture, but it is overcome by exercising patience. Applying patience removes the urge to buy now and leads to good spending habits that will improve anyone's financial situation. In chapter nine, we'll address spending habits in more detail.

Having money and purchasing possessions can bring you material comforts and some level of protection from the inconveniences and imposition of ordinary life. However, if your life is not in balance because your perspective is distorted by an unhealthy relationship with money, you need to open your heart to apply patience when you don't have hard cash to spend.

So, make the decision to not get caught in that trap of saying, "I need it now."

The truth is that exercising patience and making sacrifices is part of your satisfaction for the 'here and now' experience because it points you towards what really matters. When you consider the nonmaterial needs of others and open your heart to showing love and compassion to all, you will have started to see from this new perspective. It's what ultimately counts in life.

Patience is a mighty virtue that requires work and determination. The key to starting this part of your journey is to plan for significant decisions. Any decision, big or small, needs planning and patience. Pull back from impulsiveness and instant gratification, as this will reap havoc in your personal finances.

Have the courage to say no.
Have the courage to face the truth. Do the right
thing because it is right. These are the magic
keys to living your life with integrity.

W. CLEMENT STONE

Have patience with all things,
but, first of all with yourself.

SAINT FRANCIS DE SALES

Top 15 Things Money Can't Buy: Time.
Happiness. Inner Peace. Integrity. Love.
Character. Manners. Health. Respect. Morals.
Trust. Patience. Class. Common sense. Dignity.

ROY T. BENNETT

The Light in the Heart

Chapter 6

I have decided to ... be upright and honest.

Look from a different perspective. Develop a different attitude towards life by cultivating your moral character. In *all* of your decisions, you should be honest, upright and genuine, not deceptive or fraudulent. This equally applies to decisions about your money and possessions. Establishing a solid character is the only way you will be able to make successful financial decisions every single day.

This particular decision will tackle the very heart of our jealousies, greed, prejudice and arguments. In turn, it will move us towards our goal of a different outlook, approach and relationship with money and possessions.

Let's examine briefly what it's like to have an unethical and immoral attitude towards life. Simply put, these dishonest traits eat away at hearts that have the potential to be generous. Eventually, these behaviours destroy us, because they pull us away from our core values and we become trapped in a cycle of disconnection and dissatisfaction.

Conversely, an upright and honest attitude allows moral character and generosity to grow and increase in our hearts. This leads to joy, peace, satisfaction and financial security.

So, why are we so easily swayed to gain more through dishonest means? Already, we've seen that discontentment can lead us down this road. Another avenue to dishonesty is fear, especially the fear of lack. This particular fear has a firm grip on us, and it's extremely difficult for us to be free from its grasp. Sometimes, we're trapped by this fear because of past experiences; sometimes, it's because of information we have received. Either way, it causes us to operate in fear, and from this basis, we make bad decisions.

Let me explain it this way: Once a person defines the world or their circumstances as deficient, everything they say and do, particularly regarding money, becomes an effort to overcome the fear that there is not enough. For example, a person like this may say, 'There's not enough to go around' (deficient world) or 'I'll get this while I can' (deficient circumstances). This belief system results in fear of lack and drives people to do whatever it takes to obtain more than is needed, even if it means being unethical. Be assured of this – these actions affect the people around us, and not in a good way.

However, when we unpack the thinking behind the fear of lack and challenge the things we've been taught that have caused us to doubt, we will see that the fear is nothing more than a myth. This revelation gives us the motivation to develop moral qualities in our character, such as honesty and integrity.

Another common, fear-driven myth is that 'more of anything is better than what we have'. This myth quickens the pace of life and is the force behind greed. Yet, in the end, none of the 'more' acquired makes life any more valuable than it already is. 'More is better' thinking moves us further away from the values that truly matter and leads us on a journey with no finishing line and no winners – how can it when there are no markers to indicate when we have enough? Rather, this thinking just continues to add to stress to our lives and keeps us in financial bondage.

No matter what our economic circumstances, if we take hold of these fears as truth and believe there is nothing we can do about it, we assume a posture of helplessness. That's why it's crucial to change our perspective and our way of thinking. We must shake off our old ideas about deficiency and the need for more. The problem is that we become resistant to change when we've spent years thinking and behaving in the same way. However, this change of perspective is essential for us to develop a new relationship with money and the moral character needed to do the right thing whatever our financial situation. This will enable us to sustain the true riches, which is our relationships with friends and family. Therefore, making a quality decision to be upright and honest is definitely worth it. If we don't, we're stuck — frozen due to fear.

In chapter two, I quoted John Davison Rockefeller. Not only was he the first billionaire in history, but he was also the wealthiest person in the history of humanity (measured by today's dollars). He was a business tycoon, industrialist and bookkeeper, most famous for his role in the early petroleum industry and the founding of Standard Oil. Without a doubt, he was someone who knew something about making money. His thoughts on this subject are:

"I believe it is a religious duty to get all the money you can, fairly and honestly; to keep all you can, and to give away all you can."

Rockefeller is a wonderful example to us of someone who ethically amassed his riches. Furthermore, his words reveal that he wasn't captivated by money since he didn't obtain money solely for his own pleasure, but to give to others in need.

Maturity entails patience, integrity, honesty, transparency in relationships, commitment, love, compassion for others, and a good dose of self-discipline. If we develop these qualities in our character, there is no reason in the world why we cannot achieve a generous heart.

Consider these practical steps: take the time to examine whether you are fearful of lack. Discover where and when the fear began. Then consciously and actively work towards changing your beliefs. Make decisions in line with your new perspective of honesty and integrity, no matter what the cost.

No act of kindness, no matter how small,
is ever wasted.

AESOP (600BC – 564BC)

The greatness of a man is not in how much wealth he acquires, but in his integrity and his ability to affect those around him positively.

BOB MARLEY (1945 – 1981)

PLANNING YOUR FINANCIAL DESTINY | Chapter 7

I have decided to ... have self-control.

Look from a different perspective. Have the desire and commitment to develop and carry out a plan to reach your financial destiny. Learning to value self-discipline and achieving it in the area of finances is crucial to attaining a generous heart.

Whenever someone starts a journey, they need to decide on a destination. Once that is established, they can discover the route that will lead them to where they want to go. The same is true with our financial journey. We need to have a destination – a goal we're aiming to achieve. That goal needs to be achievable and realistic. Once we know what our goal is, we can plan our route to reach it.

Give me six hours to chop down a tree and I will spend the first four sharpening the axe.

ABRAHAM LINCOLN (1809 – 1865)

If you don't know where you're going, you'll end up someplace else.

YOGI BERRA (1925 – 2015)

Therefore, we must plan. The idea of planning is not foreign to us; we plan other areas of our lives, so it's entirely possible for us to plan to bring order to our finances, too. In fact, we have an inbuilt tendency towards order. The universe has a rule; the solar system has a control; there are laws in nature that provide order to the world that surrounds us. Society, too, tends to establish order; this is why we have laws. And we have such amazing order in our bodies that it is still difficult to understand how so much complexity can work in remarkable harmony.

That being said, let's look at the necessity of bringing order to our finances. It's essential because there is no other way to do well in this aspect of our lives. As Benjamin Franklin once said, "By failing to prepare, you are preparing to fail." If we have no plan, we will never have enough. Actually, it's surprising how well we can survive on what we have when we have a plan.

We established earlier that money is always flowing through our lives, whether like a rushing river or a tiny trickle. Regardless of the amount, when it is flowing, it can create growth, but when it is blocked or held upstream, it can grow stagnant, decay, and become useless to everyone, including ourselves. Therefore, let me repeat: if we do not plan in the area of our finances, we plan to fail. Planning our financial lives is the only way to experience financial freedom and, in turn, to live generously.

With so much information available on the subject, planning a financial future can seem daunting. The key is to learn the basics and to take one step at a time. The main problem with spending plans is that they concentrate on a typical month. In so doing, they massively underestimate what people really spend, because the plan doesn't take into account other significant expenditures, such as Christmas, birthdays, holidays, car and house maintenance etc.

The idea of a spending plan is simple. It will tell one truth – either, we spend more than we earn or that we receive more than we spend. When we know which category we are in, then we can make decisions about our finances and ask questions like, 'What can I afford to spend?' Furthermore, we must make the commitment to stick to our financial decisions. This is so important. By default, following a spending plan requires self-control. Without self-control, we may start our journey but never finish. We need to have the determination not to give up when it seems to be difficult. Self-control is what enables us to keep going, and this is crucial in making it to the end of the month.

When creating a spending plan, take into account the following:

1. A Contingency

Include a contingency to cover any unexpected expenses that may arise. This might be something small, such as an extra guest for dinner, or it might be something more significant, such as a broken boiler in the middle of winter. From either extreme to anything in between, a contingency will ensure that you're able to meet the need.

2. Savings

A responsible approach to finances includes saving, so include it in your spending plan. Make sure that your savings have a specific purpose, as opposed to savings that are for a 'rainy day'. No, your contingency is for rainy days and emergencies. Your savings, on the other hand, are to meet short, medium and long-term goals. What could you save for? Planned purchases, holidays, events, replacement of consumer goods, retirement etc.

3. Investments

Whereas savings store up money for future use with no personal risk, investments commit money into some form of investment vehicle, such as shares, stocks or bonds with the aim of making a financial return and it does include risk. Due to the risk involved, not everyone likes to invest their money, but if you have a surplus, it's worth considering as part of your long-term spending plan.

Investments definitely require wisdom, so here are some pointers. Firstly, don't invest in anything you don't understand. Secondly, invest in as many different places as you can – the key is to spread your risk by not having all your eggs in one basket. Thirdly, the golden rule is that if it sounds too good to be true, it probably is! So, stay away from all 'get rich quick' schemes. You are entering a marathon, not a sprint, and sometimes the fastest way to double your money is to fold it and put it back into your pocket.

4. *Generosity*

Plan to be generous. Money will always flow in and out of your life, so there's no point in trying to keep hold of all of it. In reality, hoarding and withholding money will affect your well-being in other aspects of your life. But by being generous, you will bless others, as well as yourself. Then, the flow of money is healthy, because it provides help and is a true gift. ***"It is more blessed to give than to receive."***

The spending plan you establish will determine your future. To put it another way, the results you experience will flow directly from the actions and plans you make ... and see through to the end. If it helps, be accountable to someone you trust.

Here are some other things to consider in your planning:

- How can you do the right thing with your finances even when you don't feel like it?

- In all situations, think before you speak. Otherwise, you may talk yourself out of your commitments.

- Restrain the urge to revert to old habits.

- Determine and plan your week. Decide how you will spend the greatest gift you have: your time.

- Prepare a budget that reflects where you want to direct your finances. This will remove the familiar, end-of-month question, 'Where did my money go?'

- Plan to reduce your debts (more details on how to achieve this are given in the next chapter).

- Take small steps.

Determining your spending habits will help you define the direction you want to take so that you will not cruise through life without any destination. It also sets limits on your financial ambitions, so that you can feel satisfied and thankful as well as focus your resources on what matters in life – relationships.

Remember to review every aspect of your spending plan regularly. Adjustability is vital because circumstances will change. An adjustable plan and a ton of self-control will not only get you to the end of the month but will also enable you to enjoy a meaningful, blessed life with affirming experiences.

Financial freedom is within your reach!

Sow a thought, and you reap an act; sow an act, and you reap a habit; sow a habit, and you reap a character; sow a character, and you reap a destiny.

ABRAHAM LINCOLN (1809 – 1865)

I tend to think of money in the same way I regard time. It's a form of energy. It comes and goes according to my intentions. The clearer my intentions, the more the money flows.

DANIELLE LAPORTE

From her article: *Getting Emotional About Money*

DON'T STRESS IT! | Chapter 8

I have decided to ... get out of debt.

Look from a different perspective. Many people dream of a stress-free life, and while there are some stresses you can't avoid, the stress of being in debt is definitely one you can eliminate from your life. Consider the following:

"When a man is in love or in debt, someone else has the advantage."
Bill Balance, American radio host (1918 – 2004).

"Neither a borrower nor a lender be; For loan oft loses both itself and friend, And borrowing dulls the edge of husbandry."
William Shakespeare, *Hamlet*.

The experience of being debt free relieves us of the stress of repayments (plus the interest!) to banks and lenders. The financial freedom that this situation provides allows us to make a difference in the grander scheme of things. When we have debts, the lender has some element of control over us, and we are in 'bondage' to them by the fact that we owe them money. The greater the number of debts we have, the greater the control lenders have over our financial position since we will always feel that we don't have enough of something to make positive steps towards a truly generous heart.

Sometimes, the 'something' is money, sometimes it is time or the belief that we cannot make a difference. I'm sure we have all had the 'I would love to ... but I can't afford it' type of conversations with ourselves. For example:

"I would love to get married, but I can't afford it."

"I would love to start a family, but can I afford it?"

"I would like to purchase my first house rather than rent ..."

"I would love to help someone else ..."

"I would love to work fewer hours and do something different ..."

Sound familiar? Maybe you have your own to add to the list.

To achieve any of these things and more, we need to invest now for a better tomorrow, and that means getting out of debt. While we will all have times when we owe money to a financial institution, we should make plans to take this stress out of our lives as soon as possible so that we can experience real financial freedom.

Remember the quote from Charles Dickens in chapter two? He gave us the golden standard for budgeting. Here's my paraphrase related to debt: Spend less than you make and you will never need to borrow! We will enhance our relationship with money when we centre ourselves on following this simple rule.

Let's look at some different types of debt and how we can be free of them:

1. Consumer Debt

These are debts acquired from purchasing two types of items: those that lose value over time and those we consume. This includes appliances, electronics, food and clothing. In the best-case scenario, we will have no consumer debt at all. But if we do, we should aim to repay the debt quickly and then plan to purchase our next consumer item without the need for borrowing. That latter can be achieved by saving. Aim to buy future consumer items with money saved for that purpose. The truth is that consumer debts are an external indication that we've been consuming more than we should, so also remember the decision you've made to be content and patient.

2. Mortgage

For many, a mortgage is the 'necessary evil' for purchasing a home. There is nothing wrong with this type of debt if we have the means to make repayments since it's a long-term investment. However, we can, and should, aim to shorten the terms and repay as soon as possible. This way, we are in debt for a shorter period of time and, therefore, we pay less interest on the repayments. Imagine not having to make a mortgage payment each month – wouldn't that make a big difference to your flow of money? This goal can be achieved by adding extra principal payments to your existing monthly mortgage amount. If it sounds impossible, the next chapter will help you. It differentiates between needs and wants, and this knowledge will empower you to focus on the areas where you can be disciplined to say 'no' to some wants in order to make extra payments towards your mortgage.

3. *Loans and Credit Cards*

Loans and credit cards are a means to borrow money, perhaps to pay for university fees, home renovations or a dream holiday. Whatever the reason, aim to pay off the debt quickly.

Regarding loans: If you have more than one, pay off the one with the largest interest rate first (it might be a credit card, so consider this), then move to the next one. It's also important not to apply for any more loans until this has been done since it will work against what you're trying to achieve. However, when a new loan is deemed necessary, make sure you have a plan in place to pay it off.

Regarding credit cards: Don't use them to buy anything that is not already part of your spending plan. This takes self-control, as explained in chapter seven. And if the use of a credit card is part of your plan, pay off the full balance every month to avoid charges.

Becoming debt free takes time and planning. No one gets into debt overnight, so getting out of it doesn't happen overnight, either. Even though some people wander aimlessly into debt, it's not possible to simply walk out of a debt situation.

If you need to get out of debt, use the guidelines in this chapter to help you create a plan, and then stick to it.

Setting goals is the first step in turning the invisible into the visible.

TONY ROBBINS

Americanism: Using money you haven't earned to buy things you don't need to impress people you don't like.

ROBERT QUILLEN

Chapter 9

I have decided to ... be a saver.

Look from a different perspective. Start to consider, understand and clarify the two concepts of needs and wants. There is nothing wrong with having both *needs* and *wants* ... and meeting them. However, to make it to the end of the month, it is essential that you understand the difference between the two and learn how to control them.

Needs are things that are required to live. For example, everyone needs food, water, clean air, clothing and shelter. Other requirements in today's economy are a good education, a good job and safety.

Wants, on the other hand, are things that are additional to our needs. Wants add comfort and pleasure to our lives.

It's not your salary that makes you rich;
it's your spending habits.

CHARLES A. JAFFE (1879 – 1941)

Don't give people what they want,
give them what they need.

JOSS WHEDON

With knowledge of this difference, we understand that we must first satisfy our needs before we meet our wants. You may believe that you can't live without name brand jeans or the latest cell phone technology – these are wants, not needs – but you can! And many people do.

The fact is that our needs and wants never end. Every day, this is evident in the lives and circumstances of people on the opposite ends of the financial spectrum. Many people live in conditions where they lack the basic needs of food, water, shelter, freedom or opportunity. Others have more than enough and way beyond what they need – they have more money, more food, more cars, more clothes and more opportunity, in fact, more of everything. Yet, these people are just as aware of what they don't have as the first group of people. This second group of 'more than enough' are consumed by thoughts and feelings of what they want to get or simply must have.

Just because our needs and wants never end, it doesn't mean that we have no control over our spending and, therefore, can never save money. We are limited only by our imaginations, which can be caught up with clever marketing strategies that transport us away from reality, causing us to *want* (not need) something that's outside of our financial scope.

Think about it: companies constantly flash their products before our eyes, endeavouring to make a sale. Realising the difference between a need and a want will help us determine when we truly need to spend and when it's wiser to save. The virtue of patience also plays a major role here.

A vital question we must ask ourselves is: How much is enough? It's very similar to the question posed in the Tolstoy's story about Pahom told in chapter one. Finding answers to this question is not easy, but we must look at our individual circumstances and determine what is enough and what is excess.

The question of how much is or isn't enough is with us every day. It is a kind of default setting for our thinking, especially regarding money and possessions. We've all seen something we want that we can't afford. Initially, it is usually a pure expression of desire, but if we haven't answered the question of how much is enough, it can evolve quickly into dissatisfaction and unhappiness. We can wrongly believe that we *need* that thing, rather than merely want it. Unfortunately, feelings of dissatisfaction give way to the urge to spend more. This is because, ultimately, our capacity to either spend or save (and, therefore, our ability to control our wants) is directly linked to how we see ourselves and how we believe others see us. Coming to a full understanding of our self-perception requires constant reflection, and it can be tough to be honest with ourselves. A person who values themselves based on what they possess will find it difficult to curb their spending, and that's why it is essential to change our perspective. Let's be clear – thinking and believing that money and possessions define us is *not* true. Money will never determine who we are, but it can control us and, therefore, seem to identify us.

So, becoming a saver, not a spender, will require a change of perspective. As with attaining contentment, this perspective change necessitates that we stop comparing ourselves to others based on money and possessions. Believe me, there are more valuable things we can compare ourselves to than other people's belongings! Perhaps you can think of some.

A saver is not caught in the marketing trap that by making a certain purchase, they are making a percentage saving. An accurate statement is that you cannot save by spending. Many 'savers' believe in the advertising campaigns that say, 'Buy and Save' or 'Save More When You Buy Now!' We cannot spend and save at the same time. The only exception, of course, is when we buy to satisfy genuine needs and the purchases made are at lower-than-regular prices.

Let's get practical about it. To become savers, we must address our spending habits. Some habits need breaking, and some need starting:

- Stop: purchasing convenience items.
- Stop: making impulse purchases that you do not need.
- Start: tracking and reviewing where your money is spent.
- Start: spending with a plan (refer again to chapter seven).

Adopting these simple habits will not only enable us to become savers, but they will also open the door for our emotional, spiritual, relational and financial wealth. This is most definitely worth the change in our spending habits.

To make it to the end of the month with our finances intact, we must differentiate between needs and wants, answer the question, 'How much is enough?' and change our spending habits. By first satisfying our needs, then fulfilling our wants if we have enough financial resources to do so, we are well on our way to becoming savers.

Now, it's up to you. You've been given applicable, practical and useful guidelines for planning, getting out of debt and saving. If you follow them, you'll become a better manager of your finances and achieve the dream of financial freedom.

There's a myth that time is money. In fact, time is more precious than money. It's a non-renewable resource. Once you've spent it, and if you've spent it badly, it's gone forever.

NEIL A. FIORE

Do you not know that God entrusted you with that money (all above what buys necessities for your families) to feed the hungry, to clothe the naked, to help the stranger, the widow, the fatherless; and, indeed, as far as it will go, to relieve the wants of all mankind? How can you, how dare you, defraud the Lord, by applying it to any other purpose?

JOHN WESLEY (1703 – 1791)

THE CURRENCY OF LOVE | Chapter 10

I have decided to ... be compassionate.

Look from a different perspective. You can be a person who prioritises compassion, love, kindness and graciousness to others over gaining money or possessions. This will require you to actively look for the best in other people, to be thankful in all circumstances and to receive help from others in your own time of need, such as a friendly hand to lift you up when you least expect it.

God gave you a gift of 86,400 seconds today.
Have you used one to say 'thank you'?

WILLIAM ARTHUR WARD

AUTHOR, EDUCATOR AND MOTIVATIONAL SPEAKER

Yesterday is history, tomorrow is a mystery, today
is a gift of God, which is why we call it the present.

BIL KEANE

We must not, in trying to think about how we can make a big difference, ignore the small daily differences we can make which, over time, add up to big differences that we often cannot foresee.

MARIAN WRIGHT EDELMAN
PRESIDENT AND FOUNDER OF THE CHILDREN'S DEFENSE FUND

Mother Teresa (1910 – 1997), nun and missionary, known in the Catholic Church as Saint Teresa of Calcutta, modelled this perspective by devoting her life to caring for the sick and needy. Her comments are for you to consider, "Let us not be satisfied with just giving money. Money is not enough, money can be got, but they need your hearts to love them. So, spread your love everywhere you go." She also said, "If you want to change the world, go home and love your family."

These powerful statements put money into its rightful perspective. In every situation, developing love and compassion is the most influential step in the transformation of our heart condition.

How do we start? By recognising that compassion is the combination of understanding a situation *and* showing love ... regardless of what has happened. Understand this: Love is *not* a natural reaction. Think about it. When someone offends us, usually what we feel is anger, hurt or hatred, but definitely not love. This shows us that *love is a decision*, not just a feeling. No matter what a person has done to us, we can still *choose* to love. Let me reiterate, love is a decision of our will. It is a conscious response, not an emotional reaction. And love is a core component in the changing of our hearts to become generous.

Whenever we give our money, time or attention to someone else, it draws us closer to that person. It might be a note of encouragement, the provision of refreshments, helping someone who is discouraged or some other kind of practical help. Whatever it may be, these actions are showing love and compassion by investing in someone's life. It demonstrates that people matter to us, that they are important, and this elevates them above material riches that seek to captivate our hearts. Therefore, making a deliberate decision to be loving and compassionate will help us to override every other thing that seeks to find its home in our hearts, including money and possessions.

Equally, when we allow possessions to dominate the use of our money, time and attention, our hearts become jealous, resentful, and we focus on ourselves, ignoring the very people who more precious than gold and silver. We would probably be much more successful at accumulating money if we were to sacrifice our relationships with family and friends, but the end would never justify the means, and we would never feel happy or fulfilled. Finding a balance between these aspects of life will take us to a higher level of personal satisfaction.

Meditate on this truth: We can give without having any love, but the opposite is not true – if we love, we will always give.

By consistently directing our hearts to expressions of love and compassion for others (irrespective of the circumstances or our relationship with them), these qualities take root in our hearts. This is important because we become the qualities we practice. As explained previously, love is a decision, so it needs to be practised regularly, even when we don't feel like it. Over time, we will not just be *doing* acts of love and compassion; rather, we will *be* loving and compassionate people. Then, we will find that our interactions with money and possessions have become secondary, and the power and control of them are lost.

Additionally, showing love, tenderheartedness and compassion toward others allows us to balance the differences between the two groups of people described in the previous chapter – those who lack and those who have more than is needed. By helping those in need, we contribute towards a better society, locally and globally.

If our sole attention is on our capacity to sustain ourselves and our families, and we do not contribute in a meaningfully way to the well-being of others, then our experience of what we have will never be nourished, neither will it grow. Believe me, we can create value where no-one would ever have imagined it possible.

What is your love relationship with money? What is your love relationship with your time? If you love or worship either, it will affect your heart condition. If you are truly in love with money and possessions, it needs to change, but it can only be replaced with a recognition of where your love and compassion should be directed, and an understanding of the position money and possessions hold in your rank of priorities.

If I give everything I own to the poor and even go to the stake to be burned as a martyr, but I don't love, I've gotten nowhere. So, no matter what I say, what I believe, and what I do, I'm bankrupt without love.

Love never gives up.
Love cares more for others than for self.
Love doesn't want what it doesn't have.
Love doesn't strut,
Doesn't have a swelled head,
Doesn't force itself on others,
Isn't always "me first,"

12:07

Doesn't fly off the handle,
Doesn't keep score of the sins of others,
Doesn't revel when others grovel,
Takes pleasure in the flowering of truth,
Puts up with anything,
Trusts God always,
Always looks for the best,
Never looks back,
But keeps going to the end.

THE BIBLE

1 CORINTHIANS 13:3-7 (THE MESSAGE VERSION)

12:07

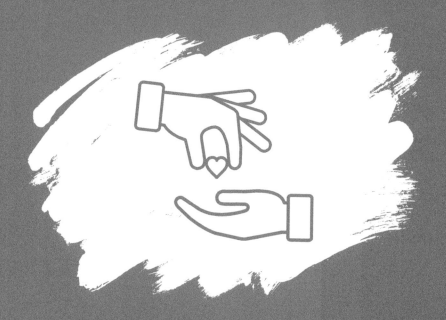

GENEROSITY: THE RADICAL CONCEPT | Chapter II

I have decided to … be generous.

Look from a different perspective. Throughout this process, you've been moving away from a heart that is consumed by money and possession towards a heart that is generous. This is the ultimate goal. Being free from the control of money will ensure that you can live a generous life.

Let's look at what this means. Generosity is being ready and willing to give more than what is expected. Although this definitely involves money, it also includes being generous with our time, belongings, ideas, admiration, appreciation and forgiveness. Interestingly, the dictionary definition of the word 'generosity' includes showing kindness, clearly demonstrating that generosity is more than just money.

We must lay before him what is in us; not what ought to be in us.

C. S. LEWIS

Letters to Malcolm: Chiefly on Prayer

Christ says, 'Give me all. I don't want so much of your time and so much of your money and so much of your work: I want you.'

C.S. LEWIS

Mere Christianity

We have looked carefully at how to develop a spending plan, and now we need to think about extending the plan beyond just money. The Ancient Egyptians believed in taking possessions into the afterlife, items such as jewellery, furniture and other treasures. What happened to their possessions? They rotted along with the people. That's why we need to look at generosity from a different aspect. The focus is not on us, but others — how we can bless others with whatever we have, be it money, time or a kind word. Since we're aiming to cultivate generous hearts, we should plan to be generous in other areas of our lives. At the end of the day, the immaterial ways of being generous far outweigh generosity with money because they build and improve our relationships, which are our greatest treasure.

We've looked at many principles about money, but there's only one rule for generosity, and that is: there are no rules! We each have the power within us to change our perspective and improve in this area of generosity. It's not every day that a person gives just to give and expects nothing in return. Actually, it is a radical idea. Let us consider it as part of the transformation in our lives, for it not only transforms us as individuals, but it also transforms the world around us. As Tim Keller said, "It is through radical giving of your income that you begin to heal the world." Go ahead. Take a step on this path less travelled. Be generous.

Greed is the opposite of generosity. It is a strong and selfish desire for something, in particular wealth, power or food. If we're going to be generous, we must be on our guard against all kinds of greed since it is never satisfied no matter how much we accumulate. As we've seen over and again, society's goal is to get more and more and more. The only antidote to this greed and materialism is generosity. To break the grip of greed, we need to do the exact opposite: give and give and give, and then rejoice and be thankful.

The problem with greed is that it often goes unnoticed. This is because, generally, we only compare ourselves to people in our social group or neighbourhood and not to the rest of the world. The human heart always wants to justify itself, so we compare ourselves to people in our social realm with thoughts like, "I don't live as well as him or her." Thus, we assess our greediness based upon our possessions rather than the intents and desires in our hearts. This was evident in the story of Pahom – he did not recognise that greed was resident in his heart; he felt justified in his attempts to improve his standard of living since he compared himself to those who had much more than he did. Please note that the story is not meant as a criticism of people who have wealth or those who desire to improve their social conditions, but it does serve as a warning about greed and its consequences. Pahom's problem was not that he wanted to better himself or his family. His problem was the greed hidden in his heart.

So, how can we gauge accurately whether we have greed within our hearts? Answering the following questions may help:

1. Am I willing to share what I have just purchased (or thinking about purchasing)?

2. What happens if my new possession breaks? How will I feel?

3. What time commitment is needed to manage the item purchased? Will it consume my essential asset of time?

Let's be honest with ourselves about whether there are still elements of greed in our hearts. If there is, we can get rid of it by being generous. Positive responses to the above questions will result in a purchase that is shared easily with others, and we will experience joy in the journey of generosity. By keeping our focus on these questions and answering them truthfully, we will use our money for the right reasons – for generous reasons. And plans and purchases will be blessed because they are made with the right heart attitude of generosity. It makes sense!

I firmly believe that resources will be in the hands of those who steward them well, that is, with a generous perspective. We *can* be generous *and* enjoy the blessings ourselves at the same time. If our hearts are in the right place and we've worked hard to succeed, let's not allow anyone to stop us from enjoying it.

* * *

While generosity is primarily about others, there's one area of generosity that we need to apply to ourselves. And that's being generous to forgive ourselves. As you've read this book, you may have realised that you've made mistakes regarding your finances, or that you've been under the control of money for far too long and have neglected your family and friends in the process. Now is the time to forgive yourself and leave your past where it belongs – in the past. A new world of financial freedom awaits you. Say something like this to yourself, "I forgive you; I love you; I am sorry for all the wrong decisions I have made; I am sorry for chasing money and for letting it control my life. I leave it behind and step forward into a new way of generous living."

Forgiveness is not an occasional act;
it is a constant attitude.

MARTIN LUTHER KING JUNIOR (1929 – 1968)

Unquestionably, you'll make mistakes again; we all do. So consider making forgiveness part of your daily rhythm. And don't stop with yourself. Be generous with forgiving others, too.

In all areas of generosity with others, give unconditionally with no strings attached for no other reason than because it's the right thing to do. Unconditional generosity will produce many benefits; conditional giving will not. There's no time like the present, so ask yourself:

How can I contribute to someone else's happiness?

How I can make my time on earth count for the people around me?

Wouldn't it be wonderful to live in a world transformed by generosity, where the uncommon is common, a world where we give with open hands and open hearts? Well, a generous world must have generous individuals, so start with yourself. Be generous with your time, money, experience and your heart. Generosity in these areas may mean that you have to be vulnerable, but don't hold back ... be vulnerable when it is necessary. When you practice generosity, your joy will overflow!

"To what extent can we give with an open hand if we haven't yet learned to open the clenched fist?" Ifor Williams, *Open Hands Open Heart*.

The world is full of people playing at half or a third of their ability. If you go out there and do all you can do, you dramatically increase your chances of winning.

A. L. WILLIAMS
Author of *All You Can Do is All You Can Do, But All You Can Do is Enough!*

If a person gets his attitude toward money straight, it will help straighten out almost every other area in his life.

BILLY GRAHAM (1918 — 2018)

LEAVING A LEGACY THAT MATTERS | Chapter 12

I have decided to ... leave a legacy.

Look from a different perspective. Many people leave legacies of financial wealth, which is unquestionably admirable and something we should all aim to do. However, in this final chapter, I would like to address leaving a different kind of legacy, one that will make a lasting difference to your family and friends.

Have you ever thought about leaving a legacy? Have you considered what it would be? Did you know that the way you live your life now and for the remainder of your years is equally as important as what you leave behind? That's because your life is your legacy. How you live now is how you will be remembered; therefore, it's your legacy.

My life is my message.

MAHATMA GANDHI (1869 – 1948)

This means you don't have to have a lot of money to make a difference. You can create a legacy now by how you live, especially by how you relate to money and the position you give it in your heart. More valuable and beneficial than any amount of money itself is to leave the next generation with an understanding of money: that it flows in and out, and that it is a privilege to be in a position to direct the flow. Leaving a legacy of real wealth is achieved *now* by valuing and honouring other people, being willing to share, inspiring others to view money from the right perspective, modelling generosity and by being a responsible steward of money. This is far more precious than the accumulation of wealth and possessions.

So, how are you living? Wisdom teaches us to get ready during our youth, during the 'summer' days of our lives for the autumn and winter that will come, when we can quit our jobs and receive financial support to do other things. It's important to note that retirement is a modern invention. No moral or physical law dictates that we need to retire at a certain age. Nobody suddenly becomes useless at sixty-five. Leaving aside health issues that could arise and situations that are beyond our control, I believe that, in most cases, the decision is yours: you can become a person who needs to be taken care of or a person prepared to live an abundant and radiant life to your last days – a person who helps and blesses humanity.

Keep away from people who try to belittle your ambitions. Small people always do that, but the really great make you feel that you, too, can become great. When you are seeking to bring big plans to fruition, it is important with whom you regularly associate. Hang out with friends who are like-minded and who are also designing purpose-filled lives. Similarly, be that kind of a friend for your friends.

MARK TWAIN (1835 — 1910)

If you desire to live the kind of life that is remembered as generous and leave a legacy that matters, make this final decision. It's a decision that encompasses all the other ones covered in this book, and it is the final outcome that will affect change in your life *and* the lives of others.

Change is significant on the outside, but real change comes from the inside out. That's the transformation this book has aimed to achieve in the lives of each reader. It's more than cosmetic; it's more than a skinnier version of the same old you! It reaches right to the heart of attitudes and perspectives, producing a new you. Yes, a new you who not only looks different but also lives, thinks, speaks and acts differently.

If you've made the decisions in this book and are committed to them, you've taken a 180-degree turn and are now heading in a new direction. You're no longer pursuing an old way of living, and you're no longer trying to be like everybody else. The new you is transformed by the renewing of your mind – a new you who is being changed daily.

I asked for strength and God gave me difficulties to make me strong.
I asked for wisdom and God gave me problems to learn to solve.
I asked for prosperity and God gave me a brain and brawn to work.
I asked for courage and God gave me dangers to overcome.
I asked for love and God gave me people to help.
I asked for favours and God gave me opportunities.
I received nothing I wanted.
I received everything I needed.

HAZRAT INAYAT KHAN (1929 − 1968)

LAST THOUGHTS

Take a moment to think about the words that St David, the Patron Saint of Wales spoke before he died:

"Be joyful, and keep your faith and your creed. Do the little things that you have seen me do and heard about. I will walk the path that our fathers have trod before us."

Sometimes, we can be so caught up in the big things of life that we forget about doing the little things. In this process of making a change, let's not ignore the little things that we should be doing. Often, the little things we do make the biggest difference. So, start small with the change.

Please note that a structure can be a helpful tool, but if we're not careful, it can become a hard taskmaster that robs us of the joy and vitality of our journey. A structure can help us to channel our thoughts and make the most of our time, but we must not be afraid to vary it, change it or even disregard it. Start your joyous journey with a blank page. I want you to know that you are not alone, life can be tough, but you can gain the joy, strength and wisdom that has helped me. My prayer for you is that God will fill your heart with a sense of excitement and expectation.

I do hope you've enjoyed **Making it to the End of the Month**. You may want to develop some of the issues a little further. If so, **Generous Heart** may be able to help.

We provide a wide range of materials and support to help you, which includes seminars allowing you to explore these principles further. A visit to our website will provide you with details of all our resources and other books, videos and programmes.

It would be good to hear from you.

Philip

For further information visit: www.generousheart.co.uk
Email: philbish1959@gmail.com

OTHER BOOKS

OPEN HANDS OPEN HEART: DISCOVERING GOD'S AMAZING GENEROSITY

By Ifor Williams

Open Hands Open Heart traces a journey of discovery, following two interwoven stories. One is the story of God's abundant, generous grace, from Genesis to Revelation, and how God teaches His people to express their love through giving. The other is the story of a young pastor, his family and church, as step by step they discover God's incredible generosity, and learn to let go and give to others. Read, be blessed, and learn to bless others.

MAKING THE CHANGE: DISCOVERING GOD'S AMAZING GENEROSITY

By Rob James & Philip Bishop

'Making the Change' is all about discovering God's amazing generosity by examining what the Bible actually teaches about the heart choice of a generous person. These studies will allow groups and individuals to learn godly principles, put them into practice and see the results of their obedience and faithfulness. Throughout four interactive, faith-based sessions, you will discover the extent of God's graciousness and generosity.

Lightning Source UK Ltd.
Milton Keynes UK
UKHW05f1308160518
322702UK00003B/39/P